half a portrait

shana jaroli

INDIA • SINGAPORE • MALAYSIA

ISBN
Paperback 979-8-89544-295-1
Hardcase 979-8-89544-566-2

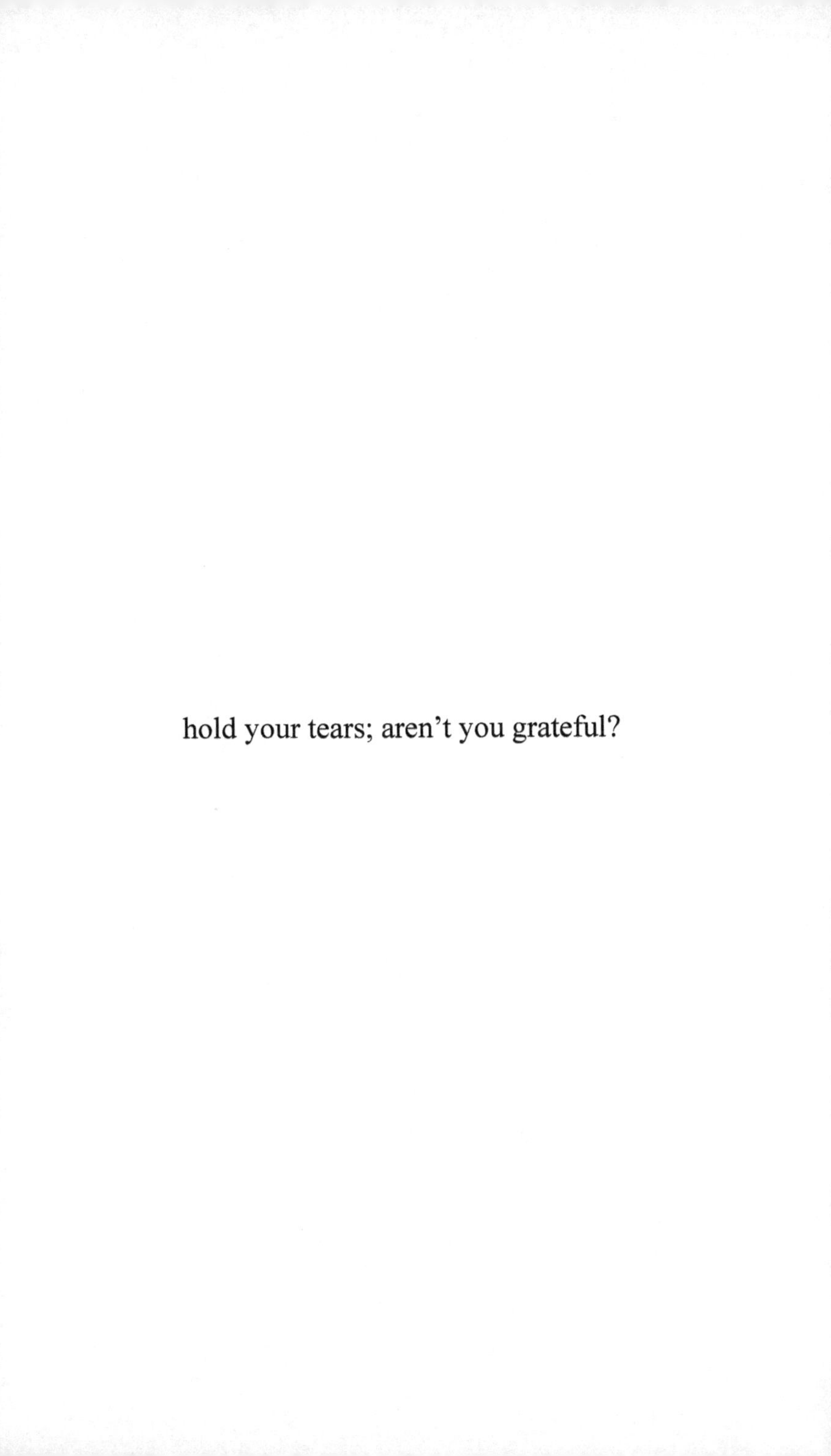

hold your tears; aren't you grateful?

would it be wrong
to spend over 20 years with myself
and still not know
who i am?

half a portrait

accusation
infinite
potential
direction
remains
definition
battle
dissolve
concrete
eternity
history
oneself
almost

i remain incomplete.

the whole concept
was to find myself along the way
but i couldn't
i didn't know which version of me
i'd ever settle for

there is something always missing
from who i have been

someone less always wanting to be more

all the love
i stored for you is boiling
in my heart
setting me on fire from the inside

all the love
i've held onto for so long
is slipping away
and leaving its mark

i am on the brink of tears
ready to be humiliated
and loved by the arms
that have abused me

life has been that way. for a very long time, i've
carried words of support everywhere with me hoping
they'll help me when i need them the most. there
are days when the words don't make sense to me.
when i have to give away some words of my own to
someone else who needs them more.

"it'll be okay"
such a far-fetched concept. when will it be? when will
it be okay enough to not walk between the two worlds
of vibrancy and monochrome. until a single word
won't shatter everything i've built silently.

how long until i randomly realise while combing
through my hair that life has been better. that i
have grown away from what was and it no longer
matters. how long until i acknowledge the colours are
colourful indeed.

how long until i say it'll be okay knowing that one
day it really will be okay. how long do i lie to myself,
to convince myself that it is the journey and not the
destination yet.

how long?

                                    half a portrait

in the longing i realize
while i stare at everything
i try to build crumbles down
that it is me who fears the change

because any amount of change is too good to be true
because what could possibly
change the agony, the failure, the turmoil
the pain i've been through

what could change what has already happened?

in the longing i realize
it is the change that chains me to the pain
it is the fear of losing myself to the change

i would return
when i am thirty
to tell the little girl
i abandoned
when i was twelve

that things might've never been easy
but i should've held onto you tighter

that i have returned to never walk away
i have returned to apologise

half a portrait

we never fit in. sometimes the absolutely perfect
things disintegrate and then with a close look we find
the cracks that were hidden all along. together, we
didn't make art. neither we had the courage to ruin our
lives for one another. we weren't madly in love. we
were just, what we were and then time passed.

the problem is, i loved harder than it was needed.

if you ever find me
crossing your mind
when you do things of mundane

would you reach out to me
and tell me all about it

would you tell me
the smell of your morning coffee
reminded you of how i liked my coffee

would you tell me
to remind me who i was
and who i should be
before i lose myself in the process?

do you believe
in another life
when the time would be right
we will try again

to fall in love
and never fall out?

right words often come from people who have wronged them and learned the hard way all their lives.

your younger self finds you
she finds out who you've become
you tell her how you became who you are

and even though she hates the person
you've become now
she tells you
she is proud of you

a woman
an account of emotions
and stories
of how everything could've turned out
differently
if it wasn't for the hurt

a woman
a word
where all the choices turn into sacrifices

a woman
waiting to snatch the first chance
to be just a girl again

the look of a half-cut, half-rotten tree inspires art. a
broken fountain stitches tales for itself. a broken jar
becomes a story of morals.

everything wrong seems right with the right words.
but where is the direction that would make my broken
heart a piece of art.

be true to yourself
where is the self?

and if i find myself
will i be true to myself
or try to run away again?

am i ready to face myself?

the touch of your hand on mine
while your tears fell through
the creeks of your golden skin
do you remember it?

you probably wouldn't
you said it wasn't supposed to end this way

but i never knew
it was supposed to end

you cried and cried
i contemplated and contemplated

i quietly left with a storm brewing inside
unaware of the harm it would spread across

i no longer have the courage to write the truth. i am
scared i'll spill the wrong words. i'm scared that i'll
change the truth and make it what i want it to be.

that is the thing with writing. it has so much room for
manipulation that it brings addiction. i write whatever
i think is right and no one can stop me. writing shows
freedom to my caged heart.

blank melodies
painful death
tasteful regrets

shedding tears
demise of our love
short lived

in all the capacity of sacrificing
i let go
i watch us
dissolve into nothingness

what were you
before you tried to become
someone who isn't you?

what were you
before you tried to hide
what hurt you?

this one morning it felt as if i could really do this.

is it really madness if i do it for love?

love blooms on possibility
without the possibility of forever
love cannot survive

would you choose them
over and over
even when you know
they wouldn't stay?

would you let it break you?

would you do it all
and say it was all worth it?

in my heart
i haven't left your side
in my heart
you were never away
in my heart
the distance never mattered
in my heart
i cried
always
in my heart
i was yours
in my heart
we were beautiful

i was talking with a friend recently, explaining the
point where i start tearing up to the soothing sound
of breeze gently touching my face, making me feel
delicate. i told them how it made me feel as if i am
something to be taken care of.

and the thought of being taken care of, the hint of
having to experience kindness first-hand always made
me tear up.

am i desperately seeking kindness, is it the reason
kindness never reaches me when i need it the most?

the suffering will cleanse your soul

it will give you the sense of direction
you had clouded
the suffering will remind you
of what matters the most
suffering will find you a journey
to the destination you've always wanted
with a bit of pain
suffering would put a smile across your face

i like to believe hate is a strong word
and everything and everyone
whom you've parted with
will not belong to hate
there are instances
where you will find peace in leaving
where there will be calm after you've left
and though it might always
feel like the calm before the storm
but it would rather be the calm
after the storm has surpassed

it will be the calm of certainty
of knowing that
nothing is going
to disrupt the peace anymore

but i only wanna come back when it hurts less.

that's what life does to you. it makes you into a
certain someone and then changes you before you
settle into it.

long nights of holding my tongue
of biting my tongue
of being careful
and not saying the right thing
the right thing being
how i felt
of putting my emotions on the breakfast table
of how i felt disgusted

between saving the right thing
and letting it go
i've lost so much
all of my words
all of my self

he is
not afraid to love
and i

i am but half

was it so hard to believe that i loved you? was it so easy to walk away from me?

so when someone leaves me, i keep holding on to them. i keep holding on hoping i don't miss them anywhere and everywhere. there is mystery in how people leave. i miss him too deeply, though i know in my capacity i'll love someone else one day. but what is pain, if not recognised and felt.

there's a tyndall effect on me
the darkness in me fades
and the world comes in sight
he is the light
he's wrapping me up with
all of the warmth he owns
he's beautiful
he's beautiful because he's sensitive
and strong
i'm proud of him
i'll take care of him
i'll hold on
i won't ruin it this time
i will say everything i have to
and every time i have to
i'll let it break me
because the tyndall is enough light
to row through the sorrow
because the tyndall is worth coming out of the grief
and becoming
a new me

in a memory
i find you
there's a light within you
filling me with warmth
you're shining enough
for both of us to make through
you're beautiful
not because you shine

but because you're here

all this time i thought i was in safe hands.
but these were the hands i barely knew.

the sides were taken silently and i stood alone.

and i wanted nothing more in the world than to hear
something rather than being silently abandoned.

don't hold me. don't wipe my tears. don't tell me
you'll be right there.

i have blamed
and constantly blamed myself
for all the terrible things i did

for all the times
i chose to walk away for myself

for all the times
i wanted to be the bigger person
but i couldn't be

for all the times
i wished i was more
but i was just sixteen

half a portrait

with a spoon full of desperation
the entire world
runs to find an identity

the entire world
strives to prove
that they know who they are
even when they cannot
contemplate what makes of them

let me find the wounds i've split open this time and
tend to them. let me save myself, stitch myself with
love before i bleed dry trying to keep you safe. let me
keep myself close to myself. let me not lose myself
again over transient hours of loathing satisfaction,
thinking i am keeping you safe.

that was some way of telling me i don't belong.
but this isn't about you.

no longer
looking
for words
just a place
to hide

now we're holding grudges
tighter than the promises we made

we grew up
time is frozen
in the memories we made
nothing of us remains
but the memories

all of our promises
are memories now

i want to be my mom's little girl again. i want to
go back home and pretend the growing up is not
taking place. i want to rest comfortably nestled in
my mother's lap. but i want to be my dad's pride. i
want to achieve everything i can to make him proud.
to tell him that all of his sacrifices were worth. i am
constantly torn between wanting to become someone
new and leaving who i was.

it is for us
to remember who we are

we are what we contain
though bruised it is who we are

have you found the balance
where you can make yourself content
without overdoing it
where you can handle grief
without losing too much

have you found the balance
between wanting to survive
and wanting to die

have you found the balance
to live?

poetry made me sad but it was all i trusted and had. i learnt my way to cling to this sadness and still be the person the world wanted me to be.

poetry was the ray of light in the days of despondence. and i knew when i understood poetry, it would understand me.

she knows
the perfect doesn't exist
yet she beats herself
every day on being less
on not being perfect

she knows
the perfect doesn't exist
yet she runs to it anyway

i could spin newer versions of myself
from a net of things, you'd prefer
i could break myself
for you
and build it up just as you'd prefer
because i'm choosing you everyday
and i hope you choose me too

and what is love
if it doesn't break you
doesn't burn you

what is love
if it doesn't change you?

there is this boy, he makes my heartache.
it is a chain of nightmares i can't seem to shake off.

i am terrified
by the fact that
i might not be able to communicate
with my future self
if i didn't write today

i am terrified
all these half-written letters
would reach my older self
and make her worry

you would think
i am still looking for you
but in reality
i am in the moments
when i had myself

the moments before
i lost myself to you

this is all about me
ever since i have known
i could treat myself better
ever since i have known
i can forgive myself
that i have it in me to do so

i am brave but never enough.
the cross connection of my past holds my present on a
fine line by a feeble thread.
i long for easy nights with lesser tears and more of
hope for the future.
but i'm a decay of what thoughts make of me.

i'm running from who i am by being who i am.

is this change, is this a fight or is this a losing war
where i give my best, lose it all and drown into
despair thinking about all the time and emotions i've
wasted.

is this a war where i lose all of my words, all over
again?

people fear the worst
they prepare themselves
and they break down as it comes
but i never imagined you
in someone else's arms
i never imagined
even for a second
to be away from your heart
because you've always been in mine
because i've always trusted you

but you were away
even when you asked
"where will i go anyway?"

you've got new memories
new friends
new stories to soothe you to sleep

and i am here
forever grieving

i could've been a lot of things to myself
but mostly i could've been kinder
i could've held myself together
when i thought i was breaking apart instead of giving in
i could've loved myself a little
when i knew all i needed was love
but the blues lingered over every road i passed by
and lights flashed in bright enough
for me to not wanting to open my eyes ever again
it is winters again, it is cold
but the cold is familiar
it is winters again and it is cold
but it has been cold since july

and i might've changed it but i couldn't
i couldn't find the warmth and it has been cold ever
since

i feel exposed to these words. words came to me when i was hurt. words i was scared to use. but this is what made me. these words helped me build my wall. these words i never gave away, these little regrets and all of my hurt, they define me.

the stronger version of love
is endurance

to have
or to not have love
but to endure through it
regardless
for the hope of love
is stronger than love itself

the extension of my shadow
reaches out to the world

i reached out to the world
but never heard back from it

while sitting
in my garden of unrealistic thoughts
i ask myself
"does the world know i am here?"

till when will you apologise for things you are not sorry about.

till when will you pretend things are okay. what is your breaking point? till when will you save the relationship that is bound to die.

till when will you say you are home when you don't even know what a home is.

to my future self
i will provide you
with everything
i deprived you of
in the past

to my future self
i will learn to be kinder to you

to my future self
i will try
to love myself
for you

i did something
that wasn't me

and since then
i haven't been able to
find myself again

half a portrait

extremes. the idea of destruction sticks with me. i'll never get enough of buying books or coffee.

love breaks you
every time you think
you can hold on a little longer
it breaks you in ways
you wouldn't even imagine

love breaks you
and the pain streams out
every time you try to put on a smile
every time you tell yourself
it is okay to let it go

love breaks you
without logical justifications

love breaks you

half a portrait

you do not need the other side of the story
to give you the answers
sometimes the other side of the story
remain in your hands
in front of you
with all the actions they have taken
to realise
there is forgiveness
only for those who seek it
not for those who abuse it

each word that you speak, that you give to this
universe comes back to you at a certain time. each
word you take out of you hoping it will fade away, it
floats in this universe with someone at some point.

                                        half a portrait

can you find shame in the corners of your bedroom?
waiting to clutch you
as soon as you return from a long day

the shame of what you've become
the shame of blurting things
the shame of breathing incorrectly
the shame of being stuck in the pattern
the shame of hiding yourself

can you find shame on your bedroom floor
where you lie down
when your tears gush?

you talk about it as if it is the easiest thing in the
world
but i remember watering a dead plant
over and over
in so many of my memories

not because i couldn't let go of what died
but because i would throw it away
and it would keep coming back to me
more broken, dying, half-alive
pleading me to tend to it

it was never about letting go
it was always about how not to let it in
in the first place

half a portrait

i could never tell, never utter a single word about the
arms that made me feel safe were the ones that i'm
most afraid of and always will be.

without the sun
the sky would be just blue

without the sun
the sky would be empty

without its sun
the sky would be lonely

half a portrait

how we travel to find the warmth
when all in truth
all in reality
the warmth is within us
we always carry it along

you go through something life altering silently and no
one knows. nor no one realizes.

and you begin to believe that when you could go
through it all alone why can't you row through it all
alone.

you blame your brooding heart for finding comfort
in shoulders of stranger than to holding oneself over
anything else.

half a portrait

but you could never make a home out of yourself
you begged and cried for help
to find you a home
when all along you could've learned
how to be the home
you were looking for

i sat under the shower
water running too fast
soap leaving traces on my body
but it wasn't soothing

the water was running too fast
almost as if i was hit by something
being pricked by needles
the soap did not leave my body completely
it burned in my eyes and i remember crying
the water was hot
not warm
skin red

i remember crying
lots of it
i remember crying
more than the soap could make me cry

i hug him and instantly never want to pull apart. i feel as if all of me is melting into him. i like that. i like not having to carry the weight of my past and present. to be empty yet feel full with his presence.

it is absurd
to believe
that the words
you overwrote the other day
will ever forgive you
why would they?
you meant them
but you couldn't own them

people find themselves in dark
and everything they have to offer
changes instantaneously

people find themselves in dark
hoping someone would pull them out of it
all the will to fend for themselves
vanishes

people find themselves in dark
losing themselves

winter on my lips. it is bitter cold in this world. this
winter has not ended for years. lake of tears. it is
paining but the sky is burning in glory of nature. the
sky keeps fighting, so do i.

fuelled by the paranoia
your heart tells you
you can try to change the ending
and you fight
you fight until you bleed blood

in the same heartbeat
you realise
something's never change
even when they pierce your heart
they don't change even when it breaks your heart

and i just don't know
how to stop loving
don't know how to give up
on someone who meant the world to me
give up on someone who's smile made my day

to not know if they are okay
to not know if they healed

i do not know
how to not give my love away

then he was just another one of my stories. another
bunch of words i read to myself when i felt lonely. he
was no more than a fantasy. he was so ordinary yet so
special to me.

i can't help but wonder
would i ever forgive them
for everything i've been through

all i had to do was find my peace
and leave the hope i cling onto
but they dropped the hope
right on my doorstep
all i had to do was walk away
but i waited
waited for the unturned promises
to be fulfilled

will i ever forgive
for the amount of hopes i was burdened by

i would not
i would never forgive

to outdo the abandonment
by walking away first
is always my failed attempt
to leave unscathed

to run away
before being stuck

without realising
i am rooted to it

does it make me weak to not want to repeat the truth
over and over because it burns my soul, crushes my
will. because it still haunts me and scars me.

is it okay if i don't talk about it every time i feel it?
will it disappear?

or will it linger around?
until every time it taps on my door i face it, sweat about it
and admit it.

i started
differentiating
when i started choosing myself

i no longer felt incomplete
in being who i was

the breathing rage inside of you
eats you

it has eaten away
generations of your loved ones

how do you beat it?
how do you beat the rage
you were born with?
that has left you with nothing?

who can you blame
for the pampered rage
that is killing you from within?

half a portrait

sadness is the melody for ears those choose to kick happiness.

writing is beautiful. it makes me feel beautiful. it is romantic. it is powerful. it is like leaving a mark, a bold one for those who care. for those who'll read, who'll make sense of everything you have to say.

winter deceived all of us
it made me stronger
when i planned to break down

it gave me hope
when i thought this is the right time
now i could give up

winter deceived all of us
having us think
things will change for the better

i didn't speak
i didn't speak because i didn't know
i was allowed to
i didn't speak because i didn't know
i could

i didn't know i had it in me to talk about it
without shattering into a million pieces
like shards of a broken glass

shards of glass that wouldn't cut me deep
when i go to collect and consolidate myself again

shards of glass that won't come in the way of
re-inventing myself

in the usual moments, i care for you. you care for me.

but the average moments of fleeting despair hovering
over you, over me.

ugly
unaware
unheard

unheard
always

and if i vomit everything
inside of me
i'll be empty

but i've always been empty
what am i holding onto?

shana jaroli

how i am so scared
of strong emotions
scared of feeling too real
scared of him wanting to have me
scared of loving again
because every time i fall in love
i end up falling out

falling back
back into darkness

half a portrait

for the longest time i was told, i was warned that the
men were not kind. i grew up learning not to trust men
with myself. and when i tried to trust a man, i failed
miserably. i was shattered into a million pieces. i was
all over the place, i was everywhere. then i learned to
pick myself up and built a new version of myself.

became the one who knew not to be afraid of men.
one who knew how to build my boundaries around
them. one who knew which men to choose, one who
knew which man would help me heal.

i told him i loved him
with all of my heart
i betrayed myself
and missed sunsets
for glimpses of him

and i'm writing in awe
of how much i was able to give
even when i had nothing for myself

half a portrait

poetry is the message half written
it is left incomplete on a purpose
it is for you to learn
and scribble on an empty page
the meaning that you'd want
that you'll connect to

i choose to love but to not be brave enough. and as i write i do not find the right words to shame myself enough.

never brave enough.
never enough.

you were wrong

you were wrong
to trust her when she said
it was okay
you were wrong
to trust her when she said
nothing has to change

you were wrong
to hurt her
and never accept it

you were wrong
to believe it was fitting
to manipulate your way into forgiveness

you were wrong
to believe
you could never hurt her

you were wrong
to believe that as you grow older
you'll outgrow
everything you've ruined

ugly scars
the ones i cannot cover up
the ones that do not decorate me
the ones that make me different

ugly scars
the exhibition of all my wrongs
of things i cannot change

ugly scars
on myself of everything
i put myself through

i cannot fix you, i cannot fix us. i cannot make it work
until i fix me. until i heal all the wounds you gave to
me, until i heal all the wounds i gave to myself in our
love.

and if i told you the unpleasant truths about me
would you care enough to stay
would you care enough to tell me
that i've been brave for too long
and now i can take a long nap

that you'll be my reality and fantasy
that you'll be the best of both worlds
and even the ugliest things won't be able to change it

how many dreams
will i break until i sleep sound
how many dreams
will i escape until i find my peace
how many dreams
until i find how not to hurt myself
even when i'm not awake

he knew the right words; she knew the right words.
they healed each other before time could.

he loves me enough to not leave me. and that's
enough for me to stay for him.

how do we speak about the stories
that ran over the course of the time
even when there was no audience to interest to

the stories that nurtured through
and lived off abandonment

how do we speak about them
without being unjust to them

and to talk about
all the emotions i was surfing on
while i fought the loneliness from lack of audience

everything in me springs to bloom
the grim in me walks past me
and july feels a little less alienated
years of hollowness turn into a field of hopes
i begin to dream
i begin to fathom what would the future hold
the presence of you
alters my trajectory of routine
i create a life
that speaks meaning
i create a life
where for every tear i cry
i promise myself a smile

wish i was satisfied, wish things didn't matter to me
a lot the way they always do. they creep on my bed,
reach my pillow on dark nights and do not go away,
ever. they stay and grow, take over and make me want
to give up.

i hold on to the little of what you give; always.

poetry moves people
but there are people
who are bent enough
by life
to write such poetry

next to the sea
anyone could look beautiful
but the ones hunting
for art would call it
too poetic
too dramatic

what we lived through
lives through us

we give space
for sadness to bloom
we give way to hating

knowingly some days
unknowingly on some

i am hunting for inspiration. being all desperate.
hoping to create something worth looking. hoping to
find it like people find love in fairy tales but can you
really find the abstract?
and when emotions are types of energy in reality why
can't my inspiration evolve from the benefit of an
emotion i possess. shifting from one form to another.

why can't i carve a way for art from the dungeon of
my sadness?

gracefully deprived.

i have a conflicting opinion
of myself
from lack of recognition
of who i am
and more towards
who i could be

i could never fully settle
on who i am

you didn't deserve any of it
but it happened
and you processed it for so long
you stood strong for so long

you have it in you to be brave

you don't own the scars anymore
but your body remembers it
you don't own the scars anymore
but in your head
they make an eternal difference

constantly like slipping sand, the memories fade away
but the stains remain.

i forgive, fade it out but never forget. part of it stays.
holding onto pieces of things that happened over the
course of smaller periods.

a mural of stains.

there will be better days
they say and i feel them coming too
but the days aren't any better
than they would've been with them
if today i am happy
with them i would've been happier
if today i smile
perhaps it is a frozen memory
of them smiling in my mind

i am because they were there

of all my attempts to
fill the void inside of me
i've failed

except when i chose you
of all the echoes i sent to
fill the void

your kindness has brimmed me
your kindness has filled every inch of my void

i find him in music, in these lyrics. all the notes reach up to me and i feel the warmth of the cold bond we shared. i don't have him but i have some part of him and that is enough to keep the pain alive.

my love for him only fuels the agony in me.

if i could pause the time
and look out for you
reach out to you and
tell you
that you've been loved
since the day you entered my life
that i have searched for you
in the space between
the falling raindrops
that i looked for you
more than you looked for yourself
when you were lost
that if the time was frozen
you'd be home now

shana jaroli

we remember certain people
with certain words
more than what the words were
we remember when they were given to us

poetry means omitting extra words. putting feelings
straight on a piece of paper for those who want
to understand. poetry is a spiral of words with a
multitude of messages to convey but those who wish
to stay unaware, dig out meanings that even the writer
couldn't imagine. poetry is both surface and deep for
the readers.

bind me or not
i will always bleed for love
love liberates me
in the sense of always having
to feel to something
to be able to choose in life

for me
love defines life

will the road not taken
lead me to who i am
or will it leave my faith dangling

is there a road
to take me to who i should be
or do i set my path along the way
and make an unknown destination
to call it a journey without dismay

a journey of being myself

this isn't about you.
but it was, everything you didn't say to my face but to
the world was about me.

did you not have the courage to talk or did you not
find me worthy enough even of your banter?

you walked all over me. made me feel pathetic, selfish
and most of all hurt me to my core.

i see through my art
i cannot lose it

the thought of not being able to make art
or even worse
not understand art kills me enough
what will i be if not the artist
to the art?

you could never know why
never receive answers
for things that have always bothered you
things you've always carried with you
because you've always been so quiet
so timid
taking care you don't sound too demanding

you've reduced yourself to so less
hoping to mean so much to others in the process

you've given away so much
to make a whole of yourself

half a portrait

i took a break from all the ache hoping it will go away eventually. but one touch to my tender heart and it all comes back flooding through the cracks of my heart to burn my mind. how i have lost at the battle of staying strong.

i have found
everything in me
to burst up into flames
and write about it
i must write before
i forget
i must make myself
sound as interesting as
i want me to be

half a portrait

that one pencil
one object
one memory
one word
that transcends you
into the realm of sugary illusions

"everything reminds me of you"

when i don't let go
the love never gets lost
it only grows stronger
with every passing minute

the sharp pain was massaging my numb head. the
headache was sweet. i wanted more of these.

tears trickle down my cheeks and i don't know what
they're for because i'm numb, so numb.

with the ravages of time
consuming everything i built
the words i gave to you
the words you gave to me
have stayed
i have loved and i have sinned
it doesn't have to make sense to anyone else

even when it wasn't beautiful
i remember it beautifully

with time
you realise darkness
can take a lot from you

also
you can give
a lot to darkness
from your own hands

how is it to live with the fact that you can't live
enough. no matter what you do, you'll stay where
you've reached and only fall back. to reach the part
of life where you've done your best and still cannot
reach the goal.

mostly
you put your heart on the line
and it gets ripped apart
and you find
the pieces of yourself
in the strangest of places

you find yourself in the randomness
trying

you find yourself not giving up

half a portrait

"you can breathe"

but i am so unsure
i always have been
all of my verses where
i find comfort
begin with a perhaps
and maybe i am doing my best
and my best isn't enough

even in the broad daylight i was lost within the
shadows of me. i am so consumed by something so
unexplainable. by something that has taken birth
but doesn't have an identity. i am so consumed by
something i cannot define, cannot understand. i am so
consumed by myself.

this distance
physical and the unfair amount of abstract distance
between us
is filled with unattended insecurities and doubts
that i wouldn't know how to overcome

i want you to know
i love you anyway
i'll love you anyway

i want you to know
without having to know all the things
i've loved anyway
without having to know
all the excuses i made to keep loving
everything i lost anyway

there are a few kind of things
he tells me
it heals me
he's probably aware of it
yet he acts as if he doesn't
he plays pretend
he shows he doesn't care
but keeps it shallow enough
for me to take the hint
i take the hint
he heals me
and i let him
perhaps i'm selfish
but perhaps has never made a life complete

every word he says
i've told myself in silence already
speaking to myself doesn't make sense
like talking to him does

i ask for all of your monday blues. when you wake
up and say you don't want to do this today. i want
to be there and help you get through; watch you get
through.

i ask for all of you when you're sick and tired and
tired and sick. when you feel nothing can save you but
love. i wanna love you and save you.

i ask to be the hope you cling onto when there's
nothing else left for you to hold on. because every day
i cling on to you. to the hope of having, you always.

we lost may
and pushed april away
we rushed for september
but all of it grew for doomed decay

we let the summers slip away
hoping to revive our lives
deep in the winters
but nothing grew from
the harshness of cold
except for the scars
those would never fade away

half a portrait

i'm consumed
by making the present okay
when it really is okay
i'm expending my energy
on things that barely
will stain my being
i'm shallow breathing
like my existence
wouldn't be defined this way
like i won't be noticed this way

no one would know i am here
no one would know how miserable i am

do you remember happy together?
the thought of having you forever never walks away.
though you've changed. though you don't care anymore
or that you did before. the thought of still having you to
myself is magical. there is peace in holding your hand.

but it is not what i want anymore. i swear. the
thoughts of you are comforting. but i don't want you
to come back. i don't want to see you and feel lonely.
don't want to see you and feel as if we could've been
because we wouldn't be what we thought we could
be. you were never enough. we were never enough
me. i never deserved you. probably you didn't deserve
me. we weren't meant for each other.

half a portrait

there's this
voice in my head
the voice isn't mine
but the words are

i do not speak them
but they come out of me

i was young
and unaware

then i was away for a while
from everyone and everything
and i grew up
rather quickly and unnecessarily

something in me died
but something in me lived
lived enough to remind me
what it was like for me to be young and unaware

it finds me still

how will i find myself on the dark days? how will i explain my dark days?

i remember sitting silent for hours unable to express my hurt in words. i remember the person on the other side of the call waiting for me to say something. 3 hours. and no words. drifted.

then i remember the days where i didn't tell anyone but picked up my pen and a piece of paper. i remember the time when it took only minutes to jot down what went across my mind.

i remember explaining myself to myself, trying to make sense of the dark days.

a capacity of a blessing and a gifted curse.

who taught you to be kind
to a world
that has never been kind to you

who taught me this form of kindness
where i try to be kind
only to myself
but never find a way into it

who taught you to be kind
to everyone but yourself?

would you clip the wings
by placing the truth
or let it fly
with the virtue of unfolded truth
it's a lie
regardless of what you make it

every night it swells up in me, the urge to scream out for all the moments i couldn't scream in. the urge to pull away myself from each and every person's life. the urge to shout and keep doing it until i feel empty enough to start again. empty enough so that new moments and memories can settle in.

i can see it happening
but not feel it in my bones

i am living all of this
without having memories to contain it
without having feelings to stick to it

i am here
but i am losing myself to who i was
and who i will be

maybe i wasn't here
maybe i won't ever will be

i am losing myself to uncertainty
of not knowing myself enough

we can steal a bit of time
from tomorrow
for today

we can take the longer route
we can be here
and watch the sun slip away

half a portrait

maybe i'll never be enough. maybe he was right.

he was so broken, i was so broken but our love, our
love was art. a sight to see.

what you meant was
you would try
not to break my heart
you didn't know
how could you

you made a promise
without knowing who you are

you made a shallow promise
built out of burnt words
and undone actions

you broke my heart
without knowing yours

half a portrait

i am a broken half
hoping the other missing half
of myself
would be intact
somewhere
unaware of what
i have done to myself

can you escape home and only return if it starts to feel that way again? is it okay to find more than one home? a multiple of places to call multitudes of home. a different place to return every time it gets overwhelming.

to build habits, to find comfort and go back to them in times of distress.

the creases of my body
remember you

the way you made me feel delicate
the way every word you softly whispered

sounded
i love you
to me

my identity
perhaps is an unfixable truth

concealed under lies
my identity
is the truth
that will never find its space

half a portrait

i wanted to feel infinite
in a way
that i could give love
like i'd never run out of it
that i could soak up
all your gloom and fill you with love
i couldn't
something defined me
a grudge

a grudge defined my love lesser. it was too late until
i realized my love was stronger than the grudges we
held. yet we held on to the wrong side of it.

what makes you
breaks you first

you reinvent yourself
by killing parts of yourself

all growth ascends
with the descent of untold bloodshed

but about words
i hope i am never over with them
i am happy with all these words around me
i am happy that i can write
and that without really expressing
myself to anyone
i unburden myself

but at times i think what will i do
when someday i'll be out of words
how will i cope up
when there will be
no voice in my throat to rely upon

it was an itch to my heart. he cared for me and i saw
him leave. i saw him leave me and then i had to watch
him leave everyone.

the walls
that i built for keeping myself safe
won't let anyone in
and won't let me go to anyone

the walls
i built to protect myself
are destroying me
from within

the smaller fragments
always fall apart
nothing stays still

nothing i make
remains intact
including myself
i fall apart
quite miserably

i end up in a lot of places
mostly never for the better
but only for the worse

the change remains
nothing else does

it stays with me, although it is the same thing,
although they're the same words i cannot stop myself
from not feeling pierced. forms of letting it out
silently reflect in my demeanour.

i'm here but nothing's new.

sometimes a moment
a word is enough
for ruining yourself

your lifetime

don't know how
but it escaped the clutch of my hands
and got past me
it's ahead of me
and i face it every day
unaware of how to win

i battle
i battle with petty thoughts
i battle with the thoughts
of losing myself in your words again
i battle with the fear of falling in love again
i battle with the fear of not knowing love
i battle with the fear
of being incapable of accepting love

i wonder if someday he'll ask me for my words and
i'll have none to offer. i wonder someday i'll have
a lot of words but none to offer them to. i wonder if
i would've ever made through if it weren't for the
words.

                                    half a portrait

you were slipping away
and i never knew how to see it
i never realised
you were slipping away
until you completely left

until you left and i knew
you never belonged to me

you were so close to me
but your heart was out of reach

maybe in some parallel universe
i am at home
lying on the floor
looking comfortably at the ceiling
thinking how i could be more

maybe in some parallel universe
i am at home
and nothing has broken me yet

and i have found a home
where i can find comfort

i watched him leave, i kept watching. i learned how to
love someone from a distance. i learned how to let go
but never learned how to walk away. so now he is not
in sight but i am stuck on the same spot. i am stuck
between all these unsaid thoughts and they suffocate.
i cannot breathe but i don't know how to walk away
anyway.

you've become a monster
a demon in my sleep telling me to run away
but i am stuck
i am stuck in the dream
unable to run away from you
i am stuck in the reality
unable to run away from you in my dream

are you, my reality?
my living nightmare?

it did not just hurt
not the paramount of pain fitting in four letters
it stung
terrible amount surging through my skin
i was losing control

i felt i was dying
except i wasn't

but the comfort of finding love between the creases of
my sheets is unmatched. the comfort of knowing that
the sip of coffee will taste better than it usually does
because it's handed over with love is unmatched. to
find love in every corner you turn to, to believe in all
kinds of love, motherly, platonic and romantic. to be
able to feel what love feels like is unmatched. to be
able to put your faith in love, to believe you're worthy
of the love that has found its way to you.

to experience love in the little things is unmatched.
to find home in the little things.

                                    half a portrait

if i could be you
and you could be me
would it be easier
to count on each other
if you could discover me
as a whole
and not just the parts you'd want
would we be brighter

i was falling all along
but you never knew
and you chose not to know
you chose to leave

if i could be you
would i have loved myself then?

swimming in the whirlpool of words
there are words here and there
among all these words
i choose the ones that cut my heart open
words by the one we love
you trust them thinking they'll not break you apart
you trust them thinking they'll understand

but sometimes strings tangle up
and it's hard to untie it
you grow closer to someone thinking
you'll seek comfort in their words
but you don't

at times you don't understand things
the way they want to explain them to you

                    half a portrait

i remember trying to grow. trying to let go. i
remember forgiving. a lot of it. i remember being
stamped on. i remember being cursed. i remember
being held back. i remember feeling betrayed. i
remember being sorry. all the time. i remember
reaching out.

i remember leaving.
i left.

my heart aches
in a million directions
it hurts because of him
it hates him
but it loves him the same
it holds him the same
close to itself

my heart is a liar
and it never listens to me

half a portrait

how will i go on
if i betray my sadness?

who will be waiting
for me next to my bed
every night if not this guilt?
you tell me
to let go but of which part
because every bit hurts
exactly the same

the sense of satisfaction
would kill my art

i cannot give up the sadness

that ache where you don't wanna lose them anyhow.

but you learn
you don't press the hurting wounds.

                                        half a portrait

how the slightest view of abandonment
reminds me of how i'm not supposed to stay
how i stayed
and never made it out of there
perhaps how i stayed and i still do
it is a scary thing
to be stuck at the same place
in the same time

i don't think
i'll ever be able to forgive you
so i'll pretend
i'll pretend i let it go
that i am fine with you ruining me
i'll pretend everything is okay even when it is not

a single sentence
loses its logic
as you grow up
logic stops sufficing
instead you find meaning in emotions

delicacy of what goes beyond. of taking a step back,
of silently being there. delicacy of holding a heart safe
even though it is not yours to tend.

i would take care of you even though you don't
belong with me. i would give everything i can to
protect you.

i am not scared of your beauty
but scared of the potential
that resides in me
to ruin you
to break you into a million pieces
and put you back up
into someone you're not
put you back up
into only half of yourself

multiple rejections
to myself
in order to accept the world

multiple rejections
at the chance of exploring myself

multiple rejections
to know beyond
of what i knew about myself
at the price of myself

some voids cannot be filled. somethings cannot be
replaced by others. somethings don't happen for a
reason and sometimes you have to believe in the
world even if it doesn't treat you right.

i've thought a lot about
washing it away
that one particular memory
of a month that plays on replay
i've thought about a mind so calm
without having to remember the details
and when you look at me
with the love dripping from your eyes
i find faith in myself to forget
to let it be gone
i find the calm to end the turmoil

you're so full of love
you're shaking
you're shaking because you have so much to give
but no one to nurture it
cherish it

you have so much of love
but it's idle
it's withering away in solace

half a portrait

remember holding the right words? it was because
you were meant to. remember not being able to back
up yourself with any argument? it was because you
were meant to. not everything happens the way we
want it to. and that is okay, it should be.

and the voice whispers to me

he might come back for you
every time he thinks he can
he will come back for you
but the choice will be mine
whether i leave with him
or leave him

half a portrait

i could write a thousand words
but never speak them
i would stuff myself with all i have to say
but never let it out
because in my head the words would have their logic
retained
but out in the open they would lose their meaning

writing is a potion that i sip every day and i don't
know what i'd do without it. writing is easy because
even if they are not listening at the moment, they can
go through what you feel later on. they can keep that
part of you in their hands forever. they can hold your
words like they'd hold you and be there without a
thought. i wish people were that easy. i wish people
would hold on to the words of each other but they
don't.

                                    half a portrait

it's winters
we walk together
to all the places and we hold hands
we're together in the moment
and it's not so cold anymore
there's a feeling of warmth returning

i lie awake
i'm awake
saving myself
from drifting away
can i do it?
will i reach back
to the shore
will i drown?

half a portrait

at 3:04am. deep into the night, is it safe to say that i
have found my rock bottom and it no longer scares
me? is it okay if i said it is a comforting place to be in.
where i have fallen over and over and no longer could
fall any further. will i find a way to plant a garden of
art at this rock bottom or will i rot away?

what happens
when the heaviness
doesn't leave your heart
when no one tells you
that you don't have to suffocate yourself
over little things
you learn that the worst part is not giving up
the worst part is to suffer
you learn that the choice
is to choose joy over madness of suffering
to remind yourself of how far you've come

you learn that when no one tells you
what to do
you push yourself to have faith in yourself

half a portrait

i was young
younger than i am now

and i wanted to be a part
of this world
desperately

i wanted to be young
and experience life

i wanted to be young
and not be responsible for everything
i wanted to be reckless
and define being young
how i wanted it to be

i just want to reach out to him. let him know that i still
miss him. and that i'm screaming into nothingness as i
have no one to understand me.

                                                     half a portrait

i do not think love is a stronger feeling than grief
maybe i'm not experiencing it the right way
but the grief of losing
of letting go
the regret of not being able to give away
what i had will somehow always
make me doubt the present

i don't want to feel limited
i don't want to write
about things that never happened
i want to be real
write about what haunts me the most
i want to write about the things
that happened with me
something profound
something that made sense
to me and me alone

you don't control
how it happens with you
but you control how to assess it

the shallow reaches the surface faster
but cannot stand it

you can't ruin a tree
by removing the branches

not until the tree
holds the capacity
to grow back from the roots

shana jaroli

every moment
where i find myself
capable of love

i am reminded
the regrets would never allow
and the mouth
would have the salty taste of tears
that i've cried over the years

half a portrait

i'm scared
i'm falling apart
this is not me
i disgust myself
i changed myself
when did it come back
why me
why can't i move on
please

why do feelings
settle back in
when we think
we've forgotten them?

i just want to be able to fall in love

what we often don't realise is
all of us are fighting for the same thing
there's no settlement for not being loved
you'll reach out
to reassurance no matter
how hard you try not to

you'll look for love everywhere you go
even though it breaks you

as artists we don't realise
that nothing matters more than
being able to let our emotions out
without breaking down and exposing ourselves
art doesn't have to be exceptional
art has to be a part of yourself
a way of saying something
creating something
that communicates through its own

as artists
the art should resonate with ourselves
before it reaches the crowd
and finds new meanings

as artists
our art should belong to us
before it belongs to anyone else

and even though
the water tasted like dust
i had no intention of wasting it
quietly
i drank all of it
strange water
i had no compulsion of doing so
but i did it anyway

human nature
to abide by
what they think should be done

i no longer
wish to be surface
but this vulnerability scares me
expressing myself
to anyone scares me

so i write half of the truth
and make up the other half
and when people ask me
i simply say this isn't me

i lie
but do i
really lie?

half a portrait

i've missed you
but that doesn't count i know

sometimes a single string
attached is enough to hold you back

sometimes a single string
can tangle you
keep you grounded to same spot

my world revolves
i write and write
until my fingers are numb
everything i write
i never read it again
i am doing everything
i can to account my life
without finding a reason
to reach back to it
without wanting to
love myself through it

half a portrait

all the promises
dissolving under our feet

i let the grudges
grow on me
grow on us

i submerge myself in water
i'm drowning

but it isn't water and i'm not drowning
i'm covered in tears
and i can't find a way to breathe

it is terrific
to imagine that someone
somewhere in this world
would be feeling
the exact same way
that we are feeling
knowing that we are not alone
that we're not the only lonely one

and every time
the scars are itchy
i remind myself
about the tree
that stands outside the door
of the place i call home
which is older than the roots
i belong to
i remind myself
if i have to stay
if i have to belong to a certain place
i'll have to face the cold
the rain & the burns

half a portrait

what will happen
if i lose
the only half of the portrait
i have

will i go back looking for me?
will someone else look for me?

will half a portrait of mine
be remembered?

in the end, she disappears.

to be able to feel is spectacular. to be able to find
yourself in the crossfire of fighting the right and the
wrong. in the crossfire of burning your childhood
but wanting to saviour the identity of it. to contain
everything you feel and to express it.

it is spectacular to immensely hate yourself yet find a
way to love yourself through it.

to call yourself a whole but only know half of the
portrait.

to not believe in the past but to pin your existence
on the future. to commit yourself into being better
without finding what makes of you.

to strive for the other half of the portrait. to give in to
uncertainty.
and to go on.

to find reasons
not to give up on yourself.

you find reasons to go on through half a portrait
hoping to discover more of yourself every time you
look for it.

i look in the mirror and ask myself,
"who are you?"

often i don't have enough words to form a single
sentence. majorly, i remain half. a part of a whole i am
yet to discover.
will i ever reach to the conclusion of who i am or will
i fight it until i can no longer fight it?

constantly i find myself stabbed, bleeding. missing
out on what happened with me.
where was i when i broke myself?

i am yet to find out what becomes of me.
until then i sit with half a portrait of myself.

-signing off
shana jaroli

shana ponders how her personality might change if she were to distance herself from all the artistic expressions she values, and the outcomes have always been unsettling for her. she's an avid reader, the author of four poetry books now, and an enthusiastic photographer. beyond her artistic persona, she is cheerful and dedicated to her work. she started her collection of poems in 2015. for her, writing was being vulnerable. 'bridges- a lost connection', 'roses and me' and 'blue butterflies' are her other books. they are a collection of raw poems composed of the feelings of her entire childhood and serves as a reminder that progress requires confronting your emotions. she hopes each of us finds the patience to witness our transformation into something magnificent, like a butterfly emerging from its cocoon. she learned that not everyone disappoints. she learned that there is good in this world, if one looks in the right direction for it. she hopes each one of us gets the courage to hold on to things that mean the world to us.

www.ingramcontent.com/pod-product-compliance
Lightning Source LLC
Chambersburg PA
CBHW021526150726
47990CB00006B/2115